ST. BENEDICT'S MONASTERY

DEDICATED TO ALL those, living and dead, who have gone before us with the sign of faith, and whose dedication and perseverence have contributed to the life and mission of St. Benedict's Monastery in its first fifty years (1956–2006).

St. Benedict's Monastery
Snowmass, Colorado

✠

Fr. William Meninger, o.c.s.o.

Photography. Br. John Ruzicka. o.c.s.o.

2005
Lantern Books
New York

2005
Lantern Books
One Union Square West, Suite 201
New York, NY 10003
www.lanternbooks.com

Some text selections are from *1012 Monastery Road*,
second edition, Lantern Books, New York, 2004. Scripture texts
are from the NRSV, New International Version and Grail Psalter.
Quotations from the Rule of St. Benedict (RB) are from
RB1980, Liturgical Press, Collegeville, Minnesota.

Printed in the United States

Table of Contents

THIS BOOK IS a celebration of St. Benedict's Trappist/Cistercian Monastery in Snowmass, Colorado. St. Benedict's was founded from St. Joseph's Abbey in Spencer, Massachusetts, in 1956. This volume has been prepared to mark the golden anniversary of the monastery, to share something of the monk's life of work and prayer, and to illustrate how the monks of Snowmass, "through daily life in our Cistercian community, aspire to be transformed in mind and heart by embodying Christ Jesus in ways appropriate to our times."

The photography illustrates the life of the monks as inspired by the two most important monastic guidelines, the Rule of St. Benedict (RB) and the Psalter.

BR. BERNARD O'SHEA
FEB. 2
1927
FEB. 15
1982

*To those who have fought the good fight
and who sleep the sleep of peace.*

FR. ANDREW JACKSON
JUNE 14
1929
SEPT. 15
1975

BR. GEORGE TAMBURELLO
MAY 8
1930
SEPT. 3
1989

BR. WALTER BRANSFIELD
JULY 15
1912
SEPT. 7
1976

BR. RAPHAEL ROBIN
DEC. 28
1924
DEC. 12
1995

Cemetery Cross

FR. THEOPHANE BOYD
MAY 20
1929
OCT. 6
2003
INTERRED AT ST. JOSEPH'S ABBEY
SPENCER, MA

FR. DANIEL KELLIHER
SEPT. 22
1922
MAR. 24
2002

Dom Joseph Boyle, Abbot

Dom Thomas Keating

Br. Raymond Roberts, Prior

Fr. Charles Albanese, Subprior

Br. John Collins

Br. Neil Gomes

Br. Thomas Johnston

Br. Benito Williamson

Fr. William Meninger

Br. Robert Brown

Fr. Micah Schonberger

Br. Jeffrey Briggs

Br. Chuck Forster　　　*Br. Dean Burchett*　　　*Br. John Ruzicka*　　　*Br. Michael Isenhart*　　　*Candidate Todd Barvinek*

These icons of Christ the Teacher and the Virgin of the Kiss were "written" for St. Benedict's Monastery by a monk from a monastery on Mount Athos. They are located in the atrium of the church.

OUR LADY of SNOWMASS

This icon of Our Lady of Snowmass was "written" by an iconographer from Duluth, Minnesota.
The Child Jesus holds the bell tower of St. Benedict's protectively in his hands even as his mother holds him.
In the background are the Rocky Mountains. The flowers are columbines, the state flower of Colorado.

St. Benedict of Nursia

S<small>T. BENEDICT OF</small> Nursia is called the "Father of Western Monasticism." He was born in Italy in the sixth century and is the author of the Rule of St. Benedict (RB), which has dominated, directed and inspired monasticism in the West since the time of Charlemagne. We know of St. Benedict by way of a biography written by Pope St. Gregory the Great fifty years after Benedict's death. St. Gregory depended heavily upon the testimony of men who had known Benedict personally.

Interestingly enough, Benedict began his monastic life as a hermit. This is symbolized in the icon by the cave in the lower left corner. He was then called from seclusion by a group of monks who wanted him as their abbot. It is noteworthy that in his rule Benedict insists that monks begin their spiritual journey by living in a community, and only when they have profited as much as possible from this kind of life ("under a rule and an abbot") should some of them be permitted to go to the solitary life. Benedict founded the monastery of Monte Casino near Rome, whence spread Benedictine monasticism throughout Europe.

This icon of St. Benedict, clothed in the black and white of the Cistercian habit, was modeled after an icon belonging to the Trappist monastery of Vina, California. It was "written" by an anonymous iconographer from North Dakota. The cave (lower left) represents the beginning of St. Benedict's monastic life at Subiaco. The monastic buildings (middle right), symbol of Monte Casino, Benedict's first monastery, are modeled after the monastery at Snowmass. Christ (upper left) holds out the Gospels that are the source of Benedict's Holy Rule.

Daily Schedule

Life at St. Benedict's is structured around prayer. We first establish the times for prayer; then we plan the rest of the day's activities. Prayer is the anchor. We begin the day with the Night Office or the prayer of Vigils, rising before dawn to keep watch for the Lord on behalf of all humanity.

A.M.

4:15	Rise for Vigils (quiet community prayer of listening to scripture and other readings)
5:30	Community meditation
6:30	Personal time for reading, study, prayer, breakfast, etc.
7:30	Lauds (morning prayer) and Mass
8:30	Work

P.M.

12:25	Sext (short midday prayer) and dinner (vegetarian)
1:20	None (short afternoon prayer)
1:30	Free time for lectio divina or a short siesta
2:30	Work or study and lectio divina
5:00	Informal supper taken in silence
6:00	Community meditation
7:00	Vespers and Compline (evening prayer)
7:30	Great Silence (until after morning Mass)

The Benedictine Legacy

HISTORY TEACHERS FROM local schools often ask to bring their classes to visit the monastery. Unfortunately, what some of them are looking for is a kind of living fossil to illustrate the Middle Ages. They are often surprised and sometimes disappointed to discover that we use computers instead of goose-quill pens and modern farm machinery in place of draft horses.

It must be admitted that there is in twenty-first century Benedictine life a certain justification for their expectations. This is to be found in the sixth-century Rule of St. Benedict, which still provides the inspiration and foundations for the daily lifestyle of the monastic community. It is evident that monasteries today do not, and indeed cannot, live with literal fidelity to the provisions of a sixth-century rule. Greeting guests with a ceremonial foot-washing, accepting infants into the monastic community, inflicting physical punishment on disobedient monks, and maintaining a prison for recalcitrant monks are but a few of the Rule's provisions that are not acceptable in contemporary culture.

Over the past fifteen hundred years there have been many reforms directed toward a renewed observance of the Rule. Usually they have had varying degrees of success, but probably none of them has succeeded in returning to a literal rendering of the sixth-century Rule.

The Vatican II document on the religious life (*Perfectae Caritatis*) calls for religious communities to do three things in their approaches to renewal. First, they must return to the sources of the whole of the Christian life; this would mean primarily the Scriptures. Second, they must return to the primitive inspiration of their institutes; this would be primarily the Rule of St. Benedict, but would also include other contemporary monastic rules that influenced it. Third, they must adapt to the changed conditions of our times. This certainly rules out any attempt at absolute observance of the Rule as written and practiced in the sixth century.

So the question must be posed, not only today but in each successive generation: What is meant when Benedictine and Cistercian monks and nuns solemnly profess to live "according to the Rule of St. Benedict"?

The Rule itself is an adaptation of a large, previously existing body of monastic literature. In the final chapter of the Rule, St. Benedict states that his rule is actually written for beginners, but, he continues, "for anyone hastening on to the perfection of the monastic life, there are the teachings of the Holy Fathers, the observance of which will lead him to the very heights of perfection" (RB 73). St. Benedict then mentions specifically the Scriptures, the writings of the desert monastic John Cassian (360–435) and the rule that St. Basil the Great (329–379) wrote in 356 for his own monastic institute. It is also important to acknowledge how deeply influenced the Rule of St. Benedict was by another source, the Rule of the Master, written anonymously some thirty years before St. Benedict's rule.

Stations of the Cross in the East Cloister

There is an increasingly popular movement among lay people to adapt the Rule to their lifestyle outside the monastery. Adapting is what monks have been doing since the time of St. Benedict, and they will continue to do so. Monks use the Rule as an inspiration, not unlike the manner in which we use the Wisdom literature of the Old Testament. The Rule is not a series of legal prescriptions or a code of law, but rather a tried and tested practical and spiritual tradition, brought into being so that we may "See how the Lord in his love shows us the way of life" (RB Prologue).

Because it is a sixth-century document, the Rule has to be constantly reinterpreted in order to be relevant to new generations, new geographies and new cultures. Thus a visit to St. Benedict's Monastery should not be seen as an opportunity to get a glimpse of the Middle Ages. This book is intended to be a reflection in pictures of how the Rule of St. Benedict is interpreted and lived in Snowmass, Colorado, today.

The entrance to the refectory. Here the monks pray the canonical hour of
Sext each day before dinner.

"Only those who are so authorized are to lead psalms and refrains, after the abbot and according to their rank. No one should presume to read or to sing unless he is able to benefit the hearers; let this be done with humility, seriousness, and reverence, and at the abbot's bidding" (RB 47).

"It is the abbot's care to announce, day and night, the hour for the work of God. He may do so personally
or delegate the responsibility to a conscientious brother, so that everything may be done at the proper time" (RB 47).

*"Brothers will read and sing not according to rank,
but according to their ability to benefit their hearers"* (RB 38).

The Books of Psalms

The Psalms

THE BOOK OF Psalms, also known as the Psalter, is the prayer book of the Church. It is also the prayer book of the monk. In the Rule of St. Benedict (RB), it is expected that the entire Psalter will be committed to memory. The psalms, all one hundred and fifty of which St. Benedict expected to be chanted each week, do present several problems. They were composed over a period of 1,500 years and express the theology, culture, aspirations, expectations and even the weaknesses of the Old Testament era. A literal interpretation of some of them is even quite incompatible with Christian teachings.

Nonetheless, the psalms are a part of the inspired word of God and therefore must be seen as compatible with the life and teachings of the Word Made Flesh, Jesus Christ. By the time of the RB, it was a well-developed practice to see the psalms on four different levels. First, there is the literal interpretation: What do the words mean as the author intended them? Second, there is the Christological interpretation: How the psalms predict the coming of Christ and how they can be seen as embodying his teachings. Third, there is the moral sense: How are the psalms to be applied to the daily life of the monk? Fourth, there is the eschatological level, in which the psalms are seen as somehow referring to the full accomplishment of the Kingdom of God.

St. Benedict was very familiar with the writings of an earlier monk, John Cassian, who explained the four senses by using as an example the city of Jerusalem. In the first or literal sense, Jerusalem refers to the capital city of the Jews. In the second or Christological sense, it refers to the Church of Christ. In the third or moral sense, Jerusalem is seen as the soul struggling to embody and provide a dwelling place for God. In the fourth or eschatological sense, the city is seen as the heavenly Jerusalem descending from above as a bride adorned in wedding garments without spot or wrinkle. Sometimes the levels are made simpler by referring to the first as the literal interpretation and the second, third and fourth as the allegorical interpretations.

For the monk, the psalms cover the entire gamut of experiences the monastic life is intended to elicit. This includes a simple appreciation of the beauties of nature, an awesome response to the power of God in violent storms, earthquakes and even wars. The psalms express for the monk his experiences of contemplative wonder and his fear of the majesty of God as well as his tender response to the paternal love of his creator and redeemer. They allow him to speak of his disappointments, illnesses, failures and sins, of his fear of the unknown and of the persecutions he suffers in his attempts to serve the Lord. No human emotion is missing from them, and they call forth every possible grace-filled aspiration.

"On hearing the signal for an hour of the Divine Office, the monk will
immediately set aside what he has in hand and go with utmost speed

Ancient antiphonary open to Vespers for the feast of St. Bernard

yet with gravity and without giving occasion for frivolity.
Indeed nothing is to be preferred to the Work of God" (RB 42).

"I thank you Lord with all my heart. You have heard the words of my mouth.
In the presence of the angels I will bless you. I will adore before your holy temple" (Psalm 138).

"To you we owe our hymn of praise, O God, in Zion" (Psalm 65).

"Let us stand to sing the psalms in such a way that our minds are in harmony with our voices" (RB 19).

"He spreads the snow like wool and scatters the frost like ashes" (Psalm 147).

Window in South Cloister after sudden spring snowfall

"Go out into the hill country and bring back branches from olive and wild olive trees, and from myrtles, palms and shade trees" (Nehemiah 8).

Palm Sunday

Blessing of the palms

Palm Sunday procession

"*Then they went to a place named Gethsemani. 'Sit down here while I pray,' he said to his disciples; at the same time he took along with him Peter, James and John. Then he began to be filled with fear and distress. He said to them, 'My heart is filled with sorrow to the point of death. Remain here and stay awake'*" (Mark 14).

Holy Thursday altar of repose

Easter Vigil

"The light of Christ has come into the world."

Good Friday liturgy

Blessing of the Paschal candle and procession

Easter Vigil

Easter Vigil in the church

"Queen of Heaven, rejoice, alleluia, because he
whom you have merited to bear has risen even
as he said he would. Alleluia."

Advent wreath ceremony before Vespers

"O come, O come Emmanuel and ransom captive Israel."

Oratory at
Christmas time

"The oratory ought to be what it is called and nothing else is to be said or done there. After the Work of God all should leave
in complete silence and with reverence for God, so that a brother who may wish to pray alone will not be disturbed" (RB 52).

Compline

The monastic day ends with the office of Compline. Here at St. Benedict's Monastery Compline follows Vespers after a brief period of silent prayer. The monks will assemble again at 4:30 A.M. for the night office (Vigils). The long interval between Compline and Lauds in the morning is one of complete silence—even to the avoidance of eye contact.

At the conclusion of Compline, the Salve Regina is sung and the abbot prays, "May the Lord grant you a quiet night and a peaceful death." The monks reply, "Amen." This is followed by a blessing of each monk with holy water as a reminder of his baptismal cleansing.

Each evening after Compline, the monks turn toward the Salve window over the high altar to sing the "Hail Holy Queen."

"Hail Holy Queen, Mother of Mercy, Our Life, Our Sweetness and Our Hope. To you do we cry, poor banished children of Eve. To you do we send up our sighs, mourning and weeping in this vale of tears.

"Turn then, Most Gracious Advocate, your eyes of mercy toward us and, after this, our exile, show unto us the blessed fruit of your womb, Jesus. O clement, O loving, O sweet Virgin Mary."

Salve window

Lectio Divina

For monks, lectio divina, sometimes inaccurately translated as spiritual reading, is an all-embracing term. It covers the entire gamut of the monastic understanding of our relationship with God. It embraces the remotest sources for prayer, starting with our experience of the providence of God in our daily lives. Anything approached with faith can be a source of lectio divina. This can include our experiences of nature, as both beautiful and awesomely terrifying; the study of science; the reading of history, novels or poetry; the blessings and tragedies of our personal relationships; and all of the other ways, both subtle and blunt, in which God touches our lives.

Lectio involves all of our faculties, physical and spiritual. It is especially directed toward focusing our intellect, memory and imagination as well as our passions and instinctual powers on the presence, activity and loving providence of God as he reveals himself to us. In a special way, lectio is presented to the monk in the scriptures, the liturgy and the writings of the monastic fathers and mothers, both old and new. Frequently these three sources are combined in the monastic liturgy, the divine office that outlines the monk's day, beginning with the night office (performed before dawn) and ending with evening prayer (Compline).

The intervals in a monk's day, those periods of time when he is not engaged either in liturgical prayer or in work, are considered lectio time (rather than "free" time). By its very nature, lectio leads to meditation, in which the monk reflects on the meaning of its content for his personal life and the world he lives in. This calls for what monks term "holy leisure," i.e. time to be alone and quiet in order to enter into an awareness and a meaningful acceptance of God's action in our lives. The entire monastic structure, or what is called in sociological terms the controlled environment of the monastery, is oriented toward providing and protecting this space. The monk must be constantly aware of the danger of allowing the "busyness" of daily labor to encroach on this sacred task.

The next step after meditatio is oratio, or prayer, properly so called. This occurs when the monk's lectio, by way of meditation, permeates his understanding, emotions and even his instinctual levels of knowing. He is then led to express this concretely in a personal relationship with God. This is expressed in the words that form his oratio, or prayer. This prayer can be a carefully reasoned, faith-inspired colloquy with God or it can be by way of formal liturgical or devotional prayers ("read" prayers such as the rosary, novena, etc.) or even at times by an effusive, emotion-laden outpouring of faith, hope and love.

The next step in the lectio process is contemplatio, or contemplation. This comes about when the physical, intellectual and emotional faculties cease to be adequate and the will (the loving faculty) seeks and is given in faith a union with God—a union that comes about in a darkness that is not the absence of light but the presence of too much light. The monk then experiences the truth of the spiritual maxim "he whom the mind cannot grasp the heart can embrace." This is referred to as the contemplative experience. In the monastic tradition these four steps (lectio, meditatio, oratio, contemplatio) are really one process, simply called lectio divina.

Suggested steps for an effective use of the Scriptures in lectio divina:

1. Build a church. Create for yourself a special environment in which you will recognize that you are doing something different and special, something that will bring you into God's presence. This can be done by going into your bedroom, closing the door,

and lighting a candle. It can be done simply by kneeling down in a private place, offering a brief prayer to be attentive to God's word, and then kissing the Bible and sitting down to listen.

2. Be aware that God has already spoken. You could not even begin this prayerful reading if God had not first summoned you to it by his grace. "No one can say Jesus is Lord unless he be given the power by the Holy Spirit" (see 1 Corinthians 12:3). You are already into your prayer. God has called you and you have answered by going apart, taking your Bible, and starting your prayer. Now it is God's turn again.

3. Allow God now to speak through the Scriptures. Open the Bible to the psalms or the Gospels. Read, listen to what God says for a verse or two until you wish to stop and respond. He is speaking to you.

4. Prayer is a dialogue. Speak to God. Ask him for an understanding of the text. Ask him how it applies to you. Listen again to what he says in your heart, the Scriptural texts, or both, and then respond again as you would in any conversation.

5. Decide beforehand how long you want to pray. Maybe ten or fifteen minutes are enough. When your time is up, thank God for his presence and his wisdom. Be prepared, when you can, to extend the conversation if you feel so inclined.

Prayer is a dialogue. It involves a give and take, a listening and a speaking. God speaks to us, we listen; we speak, God listens to us. It really is as simple as that. We must, however, realize that what God says to us is of extreme importance. We must give him the opportunity to speak and we must give ourselves the opportunity to listen.

Jesus is the Word. He is the Father's response (dialogue) to all of our needs. Through him the Father is always speaking in human accents the very fullness of what he is. He is saying everything from the fiat of creation to the bestowing of grace in all of its forms on humanity to the very final Amen, which announces the complete fullness of his kingdom. To adapt the opening of the Gospel of St. John:

> The Word dwelt with God, and what God was, the Word was. The Word then was with God at the beginning, and through him all things came to be. No single thing was created without him. All that came to be was alive with his life, and that life was the light of men.

Because God is Father, he is personal. His word is addressed to every single individual in a personal way, responding to every need in every situation. Do we need to praise God? Do we need comfort? Do we need to be rebuked, loved, reassured, chastised, instructed, pacified? God always speaks the word that we need to hear (and not always what we want to hear).

Using the Scriptures is an important and helpful way to listen to God and hear, beyond the chatter of daily life, what he is saying to us.

Contemplation

OFFICIALLY, AT LEAST, the monks of our community are contemplatives. We are said to belong to a contemplative order. But what does that mean? Part of the answer may be seen any morning in our darkened church from 4 to 5 A.M. The still figures of the white-clad monks can barely be made out scattered here and there throughout the church. Some are sitting on cushions on the floor, others more traditionally are seated in the choir. Until the clock in the cloister chimes the half-hour, there is not a stir. Then the monks arise and begin a silent, ten-minute walking meditation, covering the full circuit of the church, until they once again reach their original seats. Again they take their preferred positions and resume their meditations.

But is this contemplation? Are the monks engaged in contemplative prayer? There is no way to answer that question on an individual basis except by asking each individual monk. Certainly they are taught the principles of contemplative prayer and there is a certain presumption even before they enter the monastery that deep prayer is a part of their lives.

Perhaps there are better words to describe the monks or the monastic lifestyle. Some prefer "a contemplative attitude" to "contemplation." This extends contemplation from something done merely at assigned prayer times to an attitude of listening to God that extends throughout the day. Still others feel that "a monastic lifestyle" is sufficient. At any rate, contemplative prayer is sometimes easier to experience than to describe.

In chapters eighteen and nineteen of the First Book of Kings we read the fascinating account of the prophet Elijah and Queen Jezebel. Jezebel was the wife of Ahab, who had married her in spite of the prohibition forbidding Israelites to marry Philistines. To make matters worse, when Jezebel came to assume the throne of Israel she brought with her four hundred and fifty prophets of Baal and four hundred priests of the goddess Asherah.

Elijah was fed up with King Ahab's fence sitting. "If Yahweh is God, serve him," he declared. "If Baal is, then follow him." Then Elijah told Ahab to summon all of Israel together with all of Jezebel's pagan priests and prophets to meet with him on Mt. Carmel. It was time for a showdown.

Elijah had two altars built and told the people to bring two bulls for sacrifice. The pagans were to prepare one bull and lay it on the wood without setting fire to it. Then they were to invoke Baal to cause a fire to consume their offering. Elijah would do likewise and call upon Yahweh. The one who answered by fire was to be recognized as God.

So from morning until noon the priests called upon Baal by name, "Baal, Baal, answer us." But there was no reply. They shouted louder and, as was their custom, danced with abandon around the altar. All afternoon they ranted and raved and gashed themselves with knives and spears until the hour of the evening sacrifice. Still there was no reply, no sound, no sign of awareness.

Elijah then prepared his bull, laid it upon the wood, and told the Israelites to fill four jars with water and pour them over the animal and the wood. They did this three times, and the water ran over the altar and filled the trench Elijah had ordered to be dug around it. Then Elijah stepped forward and offered a simple prayer to Yahweh. Suddenly the fire of the Lord fell from out of the heavens and consumed the whole offering and the wood. It licked up the water in the trench and scorched the very stones of the altar and the earth on which it stood. When the people saw this they fell on their faces and cried, "Yahweh is God, Yahweh is God." At this point, Elijah ordered the people to seize the prophets of Baal, take them down to the wadi at Kishon and slaughter them there in the valley.

Ahab rushed to his wife Jezebel and told her all that Elijah had done and how he had put all of her prophets to the sword. Enraged, Jezebel sent

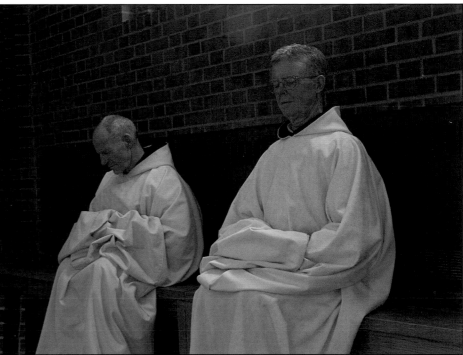

"We must know that God regards our purity of heart and tears of compunction, not our many words" (RB 20).

Elijah is the patron of mountain chapels. Here he is fed by a crow while he awaits a theophany, a vision of God, outside his mountain cave. This icon was "written" for the monastery by a friend from South Dakota.

a messenger to Elijah. "May the gods curse me," she said, "if by this time tomorrow I have not taken your life as you took theirs." Elijah was afraid and fled for his life.

But his troubles had just begun. He got as far as Beersheba in Judea where he despaired and asked the Lord to take his life. Instead, the Lord sent an angel to give him bread and water. He ate and drank and, nourished by this food, went on for forty days and forty nights until he reached Horeb, the mountain of God. (Horeb is another name for Mt. Sinai.) Elijah entered a cave and waited. He was told to go and stand on the mountain before God, who would pass by.

Suddenly a great and strong wind came, rending the earth and shattering the very rocks before him. But the Lord was not in the wind. And after the wind there was an earthquake, which made the mountain tremble and caused the stones to fall in an awesome landslide, but the Lord was not in the earthquake. And after the earthquake, fire, but the Lord was not in the fire. Then Elijah heard the sound of a gentle breeze, and when he heard it he hid his face in his cloak and went out and stood at the mouth of his cave. Then a voice spoke to him, and this was the voice of God.

Something very interesting is happening here. There is a deliberate contrast shown in the manner in which God spoke to Elijah and in the manner in which he had spoken to Moses and the people in the past. The author of the First Book of Kings wants us to see Elijah in terms of the past, but with a difference.

During the time of their sojourn in the desert, the Israelites had been a crass, ignorant people who could only be brought to God by fear and a display of his power. When the Lord promised to speak to them (Exodus 20), Moses was told to put barriers around the mountain. Any person or animal who so much as touched the edge of the mountain was to be stoned. And there were peals of thunder and flashes of lightning, dense clouds, and a loud blast of trumpets. The people waiting at the foot of the mountain were terrified. The sound of the trumpets grew ever louder, and whenever Moses spoke, the Lord answered him in peals of thunder.

Note the similarities between the story of Moses and the story of Elijah. Moses and the people were fleeing persecution from a pagan ruler; Elijah was fleeing persecution from Jezebel. Moses wandered in the desert for forty years; Elijah wandered in the desert for forty days and forty nights. Moses and the people were fed by a miracle from God; Elijah was given food and drink by an angel. Both were told to go to Mt. Sinai where God would meet and speak to them.

Here, however, the similarities end. The contrast now is quite deliberate and is repeated in three different ways. God will no longer speak to his people through fear. He is explicitly said not to have been in the wind, the earthquake, or the fire. Rather now he is recognized in quiet, in the peaceful sound of a gentle breeze.

We can take this story one step further, to another mountain at another time. On Mt. Tabor we have the same cast. Elijah and Moses are talking to Jesus. And suddenly there is a cloud and from the cloud the voice of God speaks. His command is a step further even than hearing him in the silence of Elijah. His command now is to accept Jesus as his beloved son and listen to him.

This is contemplative prayer, listening to God. Not only listening to God but also hearing him, and especially hearing him in silence, beyond words and without images.

"Besides the inspired books of the Old and New Testaments, the works read at Vigils should include explanations of Scriptures by reputable and orthodox Catholic fathers" (RB 9).

The high altar at Easter and Christmas

"Then will I go to the altar of God, my joy and my delight" (Psalm 43).

"As for God, his way is perfect. The word of the Lord is flawless.
He is a shield for all who take refuge in him" (Psalm 18).

The Rule of St. Benedict

THE MONKS OF Snowmass, as do all Cistercian monks, follow the Rule of St. Benedict (RB). This rule tells a fascinating story in its passage through time, tradition and history from Benedict's monastery at Monte Casino to St. Benedict's monastery at Snowmass, Colorado. Benedict intended his rule to reflect the monastic tradition received from the desert monks of Egypt, St. Jerome and the monasticism of Palestine, John Cassian in Gaul, and especially St. Basil in Cappadocia.

Borrowing from many sources, especially from an ancient document known as the Rule of the Master, the RB has been accepted as the normative guide for almost all western monasteries. By the eleventh century it had become the basis for the reformed monasticism lived in the great abbey of Cluny in France and in its hundreds of affiliated communities throughout Europe.

In 1098, St. Robert of the Cluniac monastery of Molesme in France and a handful of other monks, feeling that the Cluniac reform had deviated from the spirit of the Rule of St. Benedict because of an excessive stress on the liturgical celebration of the divine office, founded a new monastery near Dijon in France, known as Citeaux. This was not a reform necessitated by a laxity in the observance practiced by the Cluniacs. Rather it was an attempt to go back to the simplicity of the contemplative attitude of the Rule. Thus, there was now an emphasis on simplicity, silence, solitude and contemplation by way of lectio divina. This reform, which constituted the founding of the Cistercian order, spread widely in the Western Church until it itself fell into decline. Ravaged by the Reformation and internal negligence, the Order underwent a further reform in the seventeenth century at the monastery of La Trappe near Paris. This new Trappist reform, with its emphasis on acts of penitence rather than contemplation, quickly spread throughout Europe, establishing new houses and greatly influencing most religious orders. Since the Second Vatican Council (1962–1965) there has been yet another movement within the Trappists to return to the contemplative ideals of the early Cistercians.

St. Joseph's Abbey in Spencer, Massachusetts was one of the many monasteries of the Trappist reform that flourished after World War II and beyond because of the influence of the writings of Thomas Merton (1915–1968). From Spencer the Rule of St. Benedict was brought to Snowmass, Colorado by way of the foundation of St. Benedict's Monastery in 1956.

> *"It is the peculiar office of the monk in the modern world to keep alive the Contemplative experience and to keep the way open for modern technological people to recover the integrity of their own inner depths."*
> —Thomas Merton

The Rule is known and appreciated for its compassion and moderation, especially in view of the severity of its predecessors in the Middle East, France and Ireland. A classic example of this moderation is found in chapter forty where Benedict legislates on the proper amount of food and drink for monks. He first apologizes and admits to a certain uneasiness in specifying the amount of food and drink for others. Then, he writes, with "due regard for the infirmities of the sick" a half bottle of wine a day is enough for each. He goes on to say that monks should not drink wine at all, but "since the monks of the day cannot be convinced of this," they should at least agree to drink in moderation. The RB is intended to be a practical, concrete way to live out the teachings of the Gospels in an intense communal situation.

"To be worthy of the task of governing a monastery, the abbot must always remember what his title signifies and act as a superior should. He is believed to hold the place of Christ in the monastery since he is addressed by a title of Christ.... Therefore, the abbot must never teach or decree or command anything that would deviate from the Lord's instructions. On the contrary, everything he teaches or commands should, like the leaven of divine justice, permeate the minds of his disciples. Let the abbot always remember that at the fearful judgment of God, not only his teaching, but also his disciples' obedience will come under scrutiny" (RB 2).

Monks and Labor

IN HIS RULE, St. Benedict affirms the importance of physical labor in the life of the monk. "When they live by the labor of their hands, as our fathers and the apostles did, they are truly monks" (RB 48). Periods of the day set aside for labor are given a balanced emphasis, with time set aside for prayer. "Idleness is the enemy of the soul. Therefore the brothers should have specified periods for manual labor as well as for prayerful reading" (RB 48).

Monks' efforts to live by the labor of their hands have taken many different forms in the history of monastic houses. The most obvious and, in some ways, the most ideal form of labor is agrarian. Today, however, farming in monasteries has become almost a luxury. At one time at St. Benedict's Monastery the entire community could be seen in the fields in the evening, harvesting oats or hay, rounding up cattle or herding sheep. Today with modern farming techniques, most of this work can be done by two or three monks.

Monks have now turned to small industries (sometimes, not so small) such as baking, bookbinding, bee keeping, carpentry, even making coffins. Efforts at earning our living here at St. Benedict's have take the forms of cow-calf operations, production of hard candies and a small eggery. Unable to compete with larger commercial equivalents, we now focus on boarding cattle, farming a special quality hay for local horses, running a small cookie bakery and a book store, and maintaining a moderately sized but very active retreat facility. The monks are encouraged also to develop and express their individual interests and talents by writing, working in the carpentry shop, designing greeting cards, taking photographs, and so on.

Land is important for Cistercian monastic living. St. Benedict's has over three thousand acres of ranch land, farm buildings, hay fields, forests and pasturage. This puts the monks in touch with present-day ecological concerns and

responsibilities to the larger surrounding community. It also provides us with the opportunity to share our spacious and beautiful valley with the hundreds of guests who visit us yearly.

A "santo" from the Taos Pueblo. St. Pasquale is the patron saint
of kitchens. In the background is a rug from Guatemala.

"If someone commits a fault while at any work—while working in the kitchen, in the storeroom, in serving, in the bakery, in the garden, in any craft or anywhere else—either by breaking or losing something or failing in any other way or in any other place, he must at once come before the abbot and community and of his own accord admit his fault and make satisfaction" (RB 46).

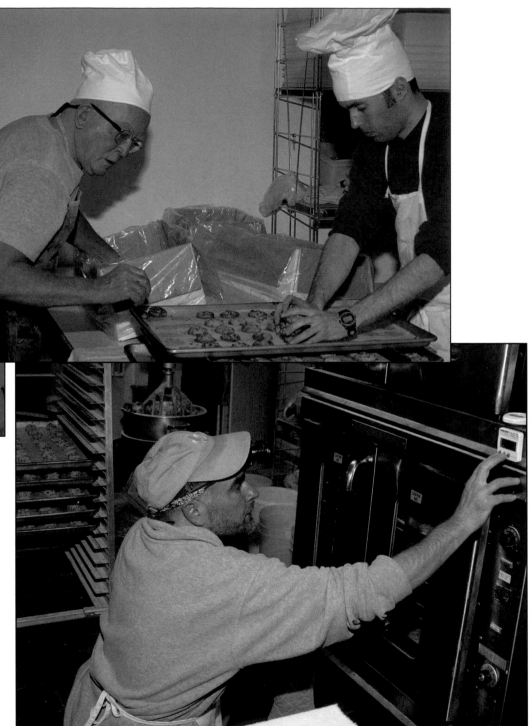

"Idleness is the enemy of the soul.
Therefore the brothers should have
specified periods for manual labor as well as
for prayerful reading" (RB 48).

"He will regard all utensils and goods of the monastery as sacred vessels of the altar" (RB 31).

"When they live by the labor of their hands, as our fathers and the apostles did, then they are really monks" (RB 48).

The monastery ranch provides pasturage for cattle and horses as well as hay for winter feeding. There are over forty miles of irrigation ditches on the ranch.

A small bakery provides work for the community in the winter, when the ranch is less demanding. Monastery cookies, each bag of which holds a "monktale," are to feed the soul as well as the palate. They are sold locally at the monastery gift shop and by mail.

The door to the guesthouse meditation room and the iron sculpture of the Annunciation were made for the monastery as gifts from local artisans.

"If there are artisans in the monastery, they are to produce their craft with all humility" (RB 57).

"The monks are to sleep in separate beds. They receive bedding as provided by the abbot, suitable to monastic life" (RB 21).

This novice is wearing a white cloak and scapular.

"The clothing distributed to the brethren should vary according to local conditions and climate because more is needed in cold regions and less in warmer. This is left to the abbot's discretion. In winter a woolen cowl is necessary, in summer a thinner or worn one; also a scapular for work and footwear—both sandals and shoes" (RB 55).

"Therefore we intend to establish a school for the Lord's service. In drawing up its regulations, we hope to set down nothing harsh, nothing burdensome. The good of all concerned, however, may prompt us to a little strictness in order to amend faults and to safeguard love. Do not be daunted immediately by fear and run away from the road that leads to salvation. It is bound to be narrow at the outset. But as we progress in this way of life and in faith, we shall run on the path of God's commandments, our hearts overflowing with the inexpressible delight of love" (RB Prologue).

Wisdom

INDIA IS OUR monastery cat, though we are not quite sure if she belongs to us or if we belong to her. I say we are not sure because there is no doubt at all in her mind. We, the monastery, the ranch, and the entire valley exist only for her benefit. We definitely get the feeling that India uses us. In her cat-mind we exist for the sole purpose of filling her dish. We are also allowed to open the kitchen door a hundred times a day for her comings and goings. Possessing nothing, she lives as owner of all she surveys, and she may well be the most integrated inhabitant of the monastery.

But then it seems that all the animals in this Eden Garden of the Rocky Mountains have the same attitude. Is this perhaps a reversal of roles stemming from original sin? Are the animals, once created to serve man, now his masters? It certainly seemed so to Br. Benito when he arose before midnight in the sub-zero February night to see if the ewes needed his help in dropping their lambs. The novices feel the same way, no doubt, when they, each in his turn, have to hurry down to the barnyard before our 4:30 A.M. night office to bring a bottle of warm milk to our first-born lamb, Agatha, who lost her mother at birth. Indeed, the normal course of our winter work day here at St. Benedict's Monastery is spent mostly in the service of "our" animals: cows, horses, sheep, pigs, and chickens.

The wild animals are no more subservient. Obviously the herd of elk, two hundred strong, that appears almost miraculously in our oat field every October evening feels that the property is theirs. Of course, they were here long before we were, but must they be so disdainful, hopping over our five-foot-high fences as though they did not exist? And the mule deer are not to be trusted either. By sheer numbers alone they lay claim to our land. After all, what can eighteen squatter monks say to eight hundred deer about living space?

And then there are the coyotes. Not only do they claim prior rights to our sheep, but they loudly howl their ownership into the night air from the fields adjacent to our monastic cells. The snowshoe rabbits and the prairie dogs own our roads. The rabbits race our farm vehicles between the road and the irrigation ditches, while the prairie dogs dig their dens right in the middle of the roads. And the porcupines! Who ever told them that we were raising an acre of broccoli just for their supper? I'm sure Br. Kevin hoped to dissuade them of this notion when he trapped eight of them in the garden last August. We won't even mention the owls who steal our piglets, nor the field mice who invade our greenhouse and try to homestead in this bonanza of succulent crops.

Red-Tailed Hawk

Horses used for mountain excursions (quarter horses)
and for sleigh rides (Belgians)

What does all this say to us? We have but to look at Psalm 104, which we sing in choir each week:

Thou dost make the springs break out in the gullies, so that their
water runs between the hills.
The wild beasts all drink from them,
the wild asses quench their thirst;
The birds of the air nest on their banks
and sing among the leaves.
From the high pavilion thou dost water the hills;
The earth is enriched by thy provision.
Thou makest grass to grow for the cattle,
and green things for those who toil for man, bringing bread out of
the earth
and wine to gladden men's hearts,
oil to make their faces shine
and bread to sustain their strength....
When thou makest darkness and it is night,
all the beasts of the forest come forth;
the young lions roar for their prey,
seeking their food from God.
When thou makest the sun rise,
they slink away and go to rest in their lairs; but man comes out to
his work,
and to his labors until evening.
Countless are the things thou hast made, O Lord.

Perhaps, after all, we are not the masters that we think we are. Or maybe we have simply misunderstood what mastery is. Is it the mastery of domination, by which we stand above all creation and demand that it serve us at whatever cost? Or is it the kind of mastery that God has shown us in the Incarnation, whereby we become part of creation and contribute to a mutually beneficial service?

What a different kind of world this delineates for us; a holistic, ecological balance in which men and women take their rightful share—one of mastery because it is one of intelligent stewardship—in which they work together with all creation.

Elk in the Basin

Marmots

Countless are the things thou hast made, O Lord.
Thou hast made all by thy wisdom; and the earth is full of thy creatures, beasts great and small.

Adam was created from the earth. He is a part of it. Raised to mastery over all creatures because he is in the image and likeness of God, he uses that dominion and reflects that likeness by exercising the very wisdom of God who tells him, "Be wise, my son, then you will bring joy to my heart" (Proverbs 27:11).

How much we can learn from our fellow creatures! How perfectly they serve the Creator simply by being manifestations of his wisdom!

Four things there are which are smallest on earth yet wise beyond the wisest: ants, a people with no strength, yet they prepare their store of food in the summer; rock-badgers, a feeble folk, yet they make their home among the rocks; locusts, which have no king, yet they all sally forth in detachments; the lizard, which can be grasped in the hand, yet is found in the palaces of kings. (Proverbs 30:24–28)

Rabbit

The ants, the rock-badgers, the locusts, and the lizard—all insignificant in the hierarchy of creation—serve God perfectly by their response to his wisdom. Men and women alone are free to sin, to be unloving, to abuse their mastery. We are a part of creation, but by reason of our intelligence we are its cutting edge. We are in the forefront and have much to say in determining its direction.

A few years ago we were privileged to receive a visit from Dr. Mortimer Adler, who summers in nearby Aspen. He spoke to us about the function and capacity of the human mind. There are, he told us, four levels of activity in the human mind. The first is information. The mind in this regard is like an encyclopedia or a computer; it gathers and stores information, a series of facts. The second level is knowledge. The mind takes the information or series of facts and categorizes them, puts them in order, and gives them organization, value and importance. (And now we are beyond the computer's capabilities.) The third level is understanding. The Scriptures tell us that "knowledge is the principal thing; therefore, get knowledge; but in all thy getting, get understanding." On this level we are enabled to live our knowledge, to have experience of it and to use it in our daily lives. Finally, the fourth and highest mental activity is wisdom. This enables us to see our information, knowledge and understanding in the light of ultimate goals, in the view of eternity, from the very perspective of God. As God made all things in wisdom, so we must see creation and our part in it from the viewpoint of God's purpose. It is surely in this sense that we may understand Jesus' statement: "The kingdom of God is within you."

This is the kind of wisdom that goes beyond textbooks and universities. It was a basic part of the life of Native Americans, who would not kill a deer for food without praying to its spirit to explain their need and their gratitude, and who would permit nothing of their quarry to be wasted. This is the wisdom that comes from the simplicity of babes and infants. Unless we become like them, we shall not enter the Kingdom of God. It is the fruit not so much of study as of prayer:

> My son, if you take my words to heart and lay up my commands in your mind, giving your attention to wisdom and your mind to understanding, if you summon discernment to your aid and invoke understanding, if you seek her out like silver and dig for her like buried treasure, then you will understand the fear of the Lord and attain to the knowledge of God; for the Lord bestows wisdom and teaches knowledge and understanding. (Proverbs 2:1–6)

"In wisdom the Lord founded the earth" (Proverbs 3:13) and it is through the wise that he brings it to its appointed fullness. This fullness will manifest itself in the establishment of his kingdom, not only in the hearts of a few simple and wise people but eventually everywhere and in everyone.

As far as the heavens are from the earth, so far are God's ways from our ways. The kingdom will not be dependent on the great and powerful of this world but on the wise, the humble and the simple. We see it now only in part and in a dark mirror, but we do see it, and we can enter into it, share it and advance it. Each one of us has his or her place in bringing about the fullness of God's kingdom.

"*Let the fields be jubilant, and everything in them. Then all the trees of the forest will sing for joy*" (Psalm 96).

"O God our savior, the hope of all the ends of the earth and of the distant seas, you set the mountains in place by your power" (Psalm 65).

"The heavens proclaim your glory, O God, and the firmament shows forth the work of your hands" (Psalm 19).

"O Lord, you have assigned me my portion and my cup; you have made my lot secure. The boundary lines have fallen for me in pleasant places; surely I have a delightful inheritance" (Psalm 16).

"Walk about Zion, go round about her, number her towers, consider well her ramparts, go through her citadels that you may tell the next generation that this is God, our God, forever and ever" (Psalm 48).

Lavabo bell tower

Monks praying the Stations of the Cross in the East Cloister

"Answer me when I call O God of my right! You have given me room when I was in distress.
Be gracious to me and hear my prayer" (Psalm 4).

Flora and fauna of the monastery ranch

"With God is my safety and glory,
he is the rock of my strength,
my refuge is in God" (Psalm 62).

"God only is my rock and my salvation, my stronghold.
I shall not be disturbed" (Psalm 62).

"You will set me high upon a rock; you will give me rest for you are my refuge" (Psalm 61).

"Sing to God, sing praise to his name, extol him who rides on the clouds.
His name is the Lord and rejoice before him" (Psalm 68).

"Praise the Lord, snow and clouds,
fruit trees and all cedars" (Psalm 148).

"He spreads the snow like wool and scatters the frost like ashes" (Psalm 147).

Scenes from the monastery ranch

Guests

Guests, according to the Rule of St. Benedict (RB), are to be welcomed as Christ, especially pilgrims and the poor. The rich, by reason of the very awe they inspire, will guarantee themselves special respect. The abbot and the entire community are told to wash the feet of the guests. Here we can clearly see how the RB needs to be reinterpreted according to the signs of the times.

It is as true today as it was in Benedict's day that monasteries are "never without guests." The RB comes from a time before motels and "bed and breakfast" houses proliferated. Commercial travelers and pilgrims especially presented monks with the opportunity to feed the hungry and shelter the homeless.

As important as they were, guests were nonetheless to be kept separate from the monastic community in order to protect the environment of prayer. Most often today guests come under the category of retreatants, i.e. not people who are in temporary need of shelter on their journey but people who come for a short period of days for spiritual renewal, counseling or reflective quiet and solitude.

St. Benedict's has a truly beautiful retreat house consisting of a large central building for guests, with a dining room, reception area and meditation chapel. There are also fourteen "apartments," most of them separate buildings in the style of a hermitage, complete with washrooms and kitchens. Thus we can accommodate individuals wishing for solitude or groups wanting to share their spiritual journeys. Guests have the option of remaining in solitude, consulting with one of the monks, or attending group conferences. Once a month there is a ten-day intensive retreat for those who have at least a moderate proficiency in Centering Prayer. Occasionally there are workshops on various aspects of the spiritual life.

"The guest quarters are to be entrusted to a God-fearing brother. Adequate bedding should be available there. The house of God should be in the care of wise men who will manage it wisely" (RB 53).

Main retreat facilities and five of nine hermitages

"I love the house where you live, O Lord, the place where your glory dwells" (Psalm 26).

"After the guests have been received, they should be invited to pray;
then the superior or an appointed brother will sit with them.
The divine law is read to the guest for his instruction,
and after every kindness is shown to him" (RB 53).

Guest house dining room

Guest cottage

Front porch and interior
of guest cottages

"Great care and concern are to be shown receiving
poor people and pilgrims, because in them most
particularly Christ is received" (RB 53).

"Once a guest has been announced, the superior and the brothers are to meet him with all the courtesy of love. First of all, they are to pray together and thus be united in peace" (RB 53).

Guest cottage

Flora and fauna of the monastery ranch

Monastic Vocations

THE MONASTERY OFFERS a place for a man—heart, mind and soul—to encounter God. Blessed to live in our majestic Rocky Mountain valley, we monks of St. Benedict's encounter God....

In the silence and solitude of Cistercian life;

In community prayer and meditation;

In the hours of private lectio divina;

In the interplay of human relationships within a small community;

In the community's work of ranching, baking, providing for guests and performing the daily chores essential to the life of the monastery;

In the instructions of the abbot and in service to one another;

In the nurturing of personal growth through the expression of God-given talents and theology;

In living out the belief that our call to prayer is an effective way to bear the burdens of the Church and the world.

Monastic life is no quick fix. It has a slower pace than life in the world, and it is directed toward a life-long commitment. Thus the discernment process is cautious, providing the seeker with time to dip a toe in the water before plunging in. Here are a few basic requirements.

1. The candidate should be a Catholic between twenty and forty-five, unmarried, and free of family obligations or debts.

2. He should be in good physical and mental health. The monastery must be assured that he can respond to the demands of close community living and contribute toward its need to earn its daily bread.

3. Since monks take a vow of obedience, the candidate must be able to live with good will toward authority.

4. The monk is vowed to a celibate life, and his need for human affection, love and friendship must be found within the monastic life according to the norms of the church's understanding of the vow of chastity.

5. One of the monk's most challenging ascetical practices is to learn to accept his brothers as they are and to be open to their criticism of his own faults. For this reason, the person who aspires to live a monastic life must be able to let go of his own ideas and preferences when the consensus of the community is to move in a different direction.

The normal entrance procedure for the candidate is to arrange with the Vocation Director for a one-week visit. By working and praying with the community, the candidate gets an idea of monastic living in general and of our community in particular. If the experience proves to be mutually positive, he is invited for a return visit, during which he shares more intimately in the life of the community.

After this, the candidate is invited to enter the six-month Participant Program to live, pray and work within the community, sharing most of the obligations and privileges of the monastery. Thus, the candidate acquires a deeper insight into his suitability for the monastic life, and the community is able to make a practical judgment regarding formal entrance into the formation program for new monks.

You may feel that, though you don't want to become a monk, you would like to live a monk's life for a while. When we have space in the Participant Program, we often accept such men. For a period ranging from one to six months you may live with the community of St. Benedict's Monastery, praying, working and sharing our life. An introductory discernment visit is for a week. Following this visit, further steps in the discernment process could lead to entry into the program. For more information contact our vocation director: Vocation Director, St. Benedict's Monastery, 1012 Monastery Road, Snowmass, CO 81654-9399; e-mail: mikamonk@rof.net. You can also visit our websites at www.snowmass.org and www.contemplativeprayer.net.

Diaconate ceremony

"Do you promise obedience to me and to my successors?"

Monks and Priests

THE PLACE OF priests in the monastic community has changed in many ways during the centuries since St. Benedict formulated his holy rule. Originally, for the most part, monks were not priests, and St. Benedict inherited the conditions that prevailed in the monastic observances that preceded him. Thus the monasteries of Pachomius, Basil, Jerome, Cassian and Gregory had whatever priests they needed, drawn from their own ranks, in order to function as Christian communities and local churches.

However, as was inevitable, most monastic communities received into their ranks men who were already ordained to the priesthood. In general, they were allowed to function according to their priestly order with the permission of the abbot. Thus, St. Benedict makes special provision for them in his rule. Unlike the immediate predecessor to RB, the Rule of the Master, which considered priests and deacons to be "outsiders," Benedict's rule did allow priests to join his community and also allowed members of his communities to be ordained.

Priests, however, were specifically enjoined out of respect for their priesthood to be examples of humility by not expecting to outrank other monks. Even though they were given a liturgical preference by being allowed to stand next to the abbot, in all other matters they were to take the rank they would be entitled to by reason of the date of their entry into the community. The priest could exercise his sacerdotal, or priestly, functions of blessing and celebrating Mass only with the consent of the abbot. He was ordered to be subject to the discipline of the Rule and not to make exceptions for himself. Other clerics (deacons, lectors, acolytes, porters) were "to be ranked somewhere in the middle," but only on the condition that they too promised to keep the Rule and observe monastic stability.

The role of priests in the monastery underwent changes as the understanding of the Eucharistic liturgy changed. Increasingly during the Middle Ages the Mass was seen more and more as a sacred activity to be celebrated for its own sake—even apart from community participation. Thus by the twelfth and thirteenth centuries the phenomenon of "Mass priests" became more common. Many monks were ordained solely for the purpose of celebrating private daily Mass, even to the exclusion of other aspects of the priestly ministry. This custom continued, with minor variations, until the twentieth century. With notable exceptions, to become a monk also meant to become a priest, and ordination was often given shortly after the monk made his solemn vows, sometimes only a few days later. Studies for the priesthood could begin as early as the novitiate.

Many of the larger monasteries became centers of study for preparation to the priesthood. Some of these even became the sources of today's great universities. Others still operate seminaries to prepare candidates for the priesthood even outside monastic jurisdictions. Since the Second Vatican Council there is a tendency in many Cistercian monasteries for a candidate to enter the monastery simply to become a monk, and the question of becoming a priest is put off until after solemn vows or occasionally permanently. Priests continue to be trained and ordained in monasteries (often after study "outside") but only to the degree that they are seen to be needed to serve the monastery in its capacity as a Christian community or church. This is a situation still in flux today and, as is to be expected, it varies in different houses throughout the Order.

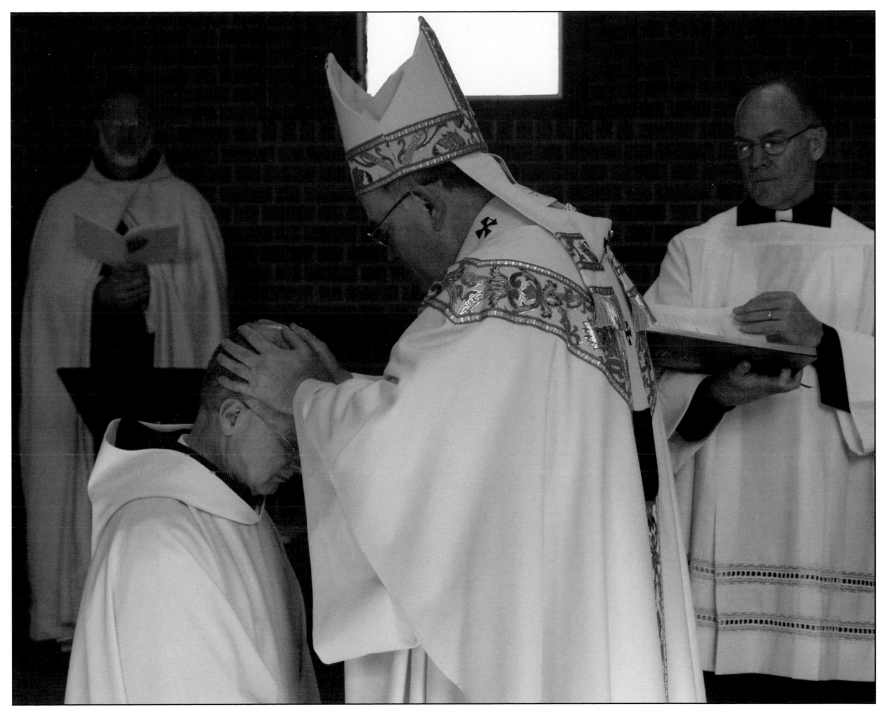

The archbishop ordains a deacon.

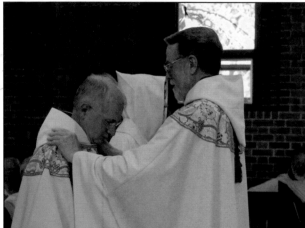

Ordination to the
Priesthood

Br. Charles Albanese, ocso
Br. Micah Schonberger, ocso

July 11, 2005
St. Benedict's Monastery
Snowmass, Colorado

Ordaining Bishop:
Most Rev. Dominic Marconi, D.D.
Retired Auxiliary Bishop, Newark NJ

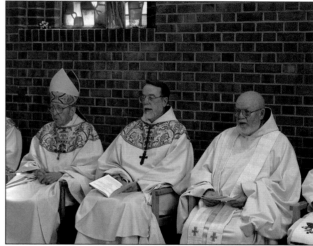

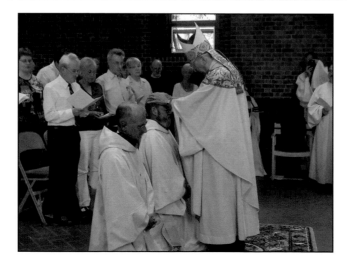

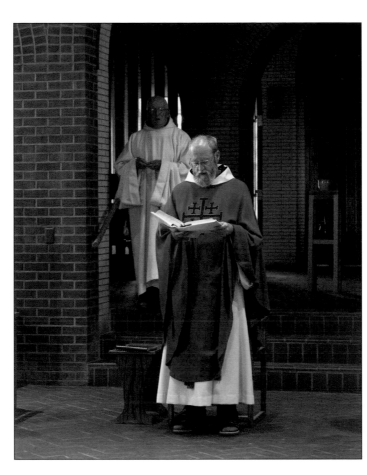

Ordinations and First Mass

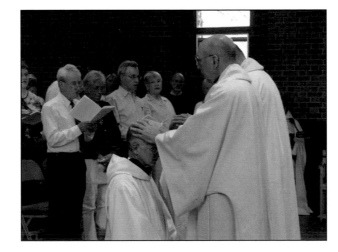

Ordinations and First Mass

Preparing for Easter ceremonies

The high altar dates from fourteenth-century England.

Entrance or atrium of the church

"How good and pleasant it is when brothers live together in unity" (Psalm 133).

Birthday celebrations are always special.

Archetype Monk

THERE IS AN organization in Aspen, Colorado called the Aspen Institute for Humanistic Studies. Founded by the philosopher Mortimer Adler, it periodically calls together executives from businesses all over the world to meet and discuss the humanities, philosophy, religion and ethics—in other words, subjects that they as businessmen and -women are not usually exposed to. Often, as a part of the "Aspen experience," these groups make a visit to our monastery to attend our evening Vespers and Eucharistic liturgy, and to chat with the monks about our "alternative lifestyle." Most of them are not Catholic and have never before visited a monastery.

A letter received recently from an IBM executive after one such visit stated: "I am not a Catholic, possibly not even a Christian. I have never visited a monastery before and do not completely understand what I saw there or how it has affected me, but I know I am permanently changed—and for the better." Why is this? Why should a single brief visit to a monastery have such a powerful effect? Why are people so fascinated by monks and by things monastic?

One evening, Fr. Theophane and I met with a group from the Aspen Institute. They seemed to be interested in every aspect of monastic living, and the questions were coming fast and furious long after the time allotted had expired. Taking advantage of a brief pause in the barrage of questions, Fr. Theophane remarked: "See how interested you all are in the monastic life. There is a reason for this. Something of the monk exists in every one of us." I think this is a statement of profound truth. According to Carl Jung, there exist in all of us myths or archetypes that are the forms whereby our collective unconscious represents for itself the fundamental meanings of our basic relationships. Thus there exists in each one of us something of the Man, the Woman, the King, the Evil One, the Monk, etc. It is this element of the Monk in each of us that resonates with the silence, austerity, prayer, poverty, simplicity and obedience somehow tasted in even a brief visit to a monastery.

The days are gone when the whole Church saw the monastic life as her ideal model. There are many other models, spiritualities, or theological systems that relate more and more authentically to life in this modern world. Yet monastic spirituality will always have its place. It will always speak to something that lies deep in the innermost being of every man and woman of every culture and religious belief. The Franciscan Liberation Theologian, Leonardo Boff, says that Jesus will not allow himself to be domesticated by any particular theological system. What Jesus tells us of God is too great to be comprehended and explained by any one form of spirituality. Jesus is the Word that must be spoken over and over again in every age, to every people, and in every

write books and even occasionally leave our monasteries to give conferences, workshops and retreats. But above all, our witness is in the living, in the abiding communal expression of the contemplative attitude.

culture. He is colored by every situation (so Jesus is black in Africa, yellow in Asia, white in Europe), fully expressed by none, touched upon by all.

Yet there is something of the Word that is Jesus that is spoken in the center of our beings and that reaches a recognizable expression in the monastic life. This is why monasticism is a viable witness and why encountering this witness elicits such a resonating response in the hearts of so many men and women.

For some the words "monastic" and "contemplative" are almost synonymous. To be a monk is to be a contemplative, to bear witness to the value of contemplation and to share this value with those who resonate with it and wish to support and strengthen it in themselves. This sharing is indeed a viable part of monastic spirituality, and is the reason why we Trappist monks

The Goal of Monastic Life

WHAT IS THE primary goal of the monastic life? In the past ten years, I have interviewed scores of potential candidates for vocations. Fifty years ago, if someone came to the monastery to save his soul or to do penance for his sins, he would have been accepted without question. Today, such motives are held in suspicion—not that they are necessarily wrong, but because there are higher motivations and more authentic expressions of them that are expected today. Monastic aspirations are now expressed more in terms of loving God and desiring to seek him to the exclusion of all else, or articulated in terms of aspiring to a set of values to be pursued in a supportive community that gives witness to desiring and seeking those same values. The notion of becoming a monk because one desires heaven or fears hell is not totally absent, but it is not a dominant reason for life-choices.

People today are more human-centered than God-centered. This does not mean, as it may seem, that God takes second place to human beings. What it does mean is that God takes first place in the human rather than over the human. This is one of the basic assumptions of Liberation Theology, and it is becoming more and more an expression of the thought-patterns and motivational rationale of our young people. It is a direct result of the theological conclusions stemming from the doctrine of the Incarnation and the specific teachings of Jesus himself as expressed in the Gospels.

Where should the priority lie? What is more important, our service to one another during this life or the successful achievement of the ultimate goal of our salvation, which is eternal life with God in heaven? The two questions are, in reality, one, and the answers to both of them need not be contradictory.

Theology, like every science, has many branches. Monasticism is very much concerned with that branch called eschatology. Literally, eschatology refers to the study of the last things, specifically: death, judgment, heaven, hell. Monks are supposed to be already living the heavenly life—although not in any unrealistic sense. Monastic faith is supposed to be so strong that monks live as though the veil of faith were lifted and they find themselves constantly in God's presence. Likewise their hope is supposed to be so strong that, in a sense, they already have the fulfillment of God's presence.

This is why monastic vows are not sacraments. A sacrament is a sign. Monastic consecration is supposed to be the reality itself. In monastic poverty, monks own nothing specifically, but all that God has created is theirs. In monastic celibacy, monks do not have children or wives, but are "as angels in heaven." In monastic obedience, they find the will of God.

In the past few decades, a fascinating element of eschatology has come to the fore. Due in large part to the great scriptural work of scholar and humanitarian Albert Schweitzer (1875–1965), we have realized since the beginning of the twentieth century the primary place of eschatology in the New Testament. Theological speculation, influenced by this principle, has come up with some rich and wide-ranging ideas. It has been called a rediscovery of the eschatological dimension of Christian revelation. If it affects revelation, it must have significant repercussions on Christian existence. The Swiss theologian Karl Barth (1886–1968) refers to the objects of eschatology as the "ultimate realities" and claims that they are the first principles of everything. Contemporary Liberation Theologian Gustavo Gutierrez goes even further, stressing how the eschatological theme continues to grow in our understanding of God's message today. He calls eschatology the "driving force" of salvific history. For him, it is not just another branch of theology, but the very heart of living and the key to understanding Christian revelation.

To understand eschatology as referring only to the last things is not enough. Extra-historical events such as the end of the world, the Second Coming, and the Last Judgment are of great import to Christians and, indeed, to all humanity, whether people believe in them or not. However, these great mysteries

must be seen not as some far-off eventualities known only through faith, but as powerful incentives, divine goals, and even cosmic energetic forces calling into being our present-day activities and influencing them in the form and direction of God's eternal plan. All of our present-day events must be directed toward and worthy of "the new city of God coming down from heaven." (See Revelation 21:2.)

This driving impulse toward the future is grace, bestowing meaning, value, and divine direction to the present. As Gutierrez puts it, "The attraction of what is to come is the driving force of history. The action of Yahweh in history and his action at the end of history are inseparable" (*A Theology of Liberation,* NY: Orbis, 1973, p. 164). We can only understand the real meaning of God's interventions in salvation history and in our own lives when we see that history and those lives from their eschatological perspective.

The future influences the present. The eternal now of God interfaces our past, present, and future, and reveals to us a value and significance in our activity that far exceeds the limited visions of the most farseeing prophets. History can no longer be seen as a record of the past; it is, rather, a "thrust into the future."

Monastic life receives its hope and joy from the expectation that eschatology thrusts upon it. The future hope of the world, stemming from God's promises, incarnated in the divine Word and given living force in the activity of the Holy Spirit, has its roots in the present, giving meaning to our labors, and calling forth joyous eschatological celebration.

God's ways are not our ways, yet it remains paradoxically true that the divine Word has leapt into our midst and gives us a share in his own divine life. Somehow the task we have received from Adam to carry on the work of caring for the earth is going to result, not in another tower of Babel, but in the heavenly Jerusalem. The life force motivating and informing this process from creation to New Creation is God himself manifested as the Pentecostal life-giving Spirit, living among us as the Spirit of Christ, the bond and soul of his Mystical Body, and concretely manifesting himself in every act of genuine love brought forth on this earth.

Through all of this, then, monastic spirituality is informed, inspired and motivated. The liturgical expression of monastic eschatological hope is the night office, or, as it is more aptly called, Vigils. Arising hours before dawn, monastic communities await in silent prayer, meditative readings, and psalmody the coming of Christ as symbolized by the rising sun. In faith and hope, the eschatological coming of Christ "on the clouds and in glory" (see Matthew 24:30) is anticipated and somehow grasped and realized on a daily basis. The future is thrust into the present.

This hundred-year-old farmhouse was used as the original monastery in 1956 while the monks were constructing the present buildings.

History of the Monastery

Fr. Micah Schonberger, o.c.s.o.

Duration the French Revolution and, in general, the eighteenth century, Europe cast a negative eye on Catholic religious orders. As a result, the monasteries in France were closed and confiscated, and the monks and nuns dispersed. With the dissolution of monasteries in France, survival of the Cistercian Order depended on an incredible exodus of monks from the French monastery of La Trappe (hence the name "Trappist" for our Order). Led by their novice master, Fr. Augustine de Lestrange, a group of monks, along with a group of French Cistercian nuns, sought refuge in an abandoned Carthusian monastery in Switzerland, where they followed a remarkably austere life. From Switzerland they moved from one country to another, traveling as far as Russia and, eventually, back to France, following Napoleon's defeat and exile. In 1803, while they were still in Switzerland, Lestrange sent twenty monks to North America to make a foundation. After a discouraging eleven-year struggle, these monks returned to a post-Napoleonic France less hostile to the Church.

However, one monk, Fr. Vincent de Paul Merle (1768–1853), was left behind in Halifax, Nova Scotia in May 1815. While serving as a priest in the diocese of present day Antigonish, he located a tract of land that he thought was suitable for establishing a monastery. He then arranged with Fr. Lestrange, now living at the French monastery of Bellefontaine, to begin the New World foundation of Petit Clairvaux. The little community began with only five monks. Though less extreme than that of Lestrange's nomadic group, the highly ascetical life that was the hallmark of the Trappists proved too rigorous to attract many local candidates. They struggled for nearly forty years until, in 1857, the Belgian monastery of Saint Sixtus sent eighteen monks to help the surviving community work the land according to the custom of their European forerunners since medieval times.

In 1869, Petit Clairvaux was admitted into the Cistercian Order. It chose to align itself with those monasteries within the Order that observed the reforms inaugurated at the Cistercian monastery of La Trappe. By 1876 the fledgling monastery had grown sufficiently stable to become self-governing and to elect its first abbot. In 1882, the French Cistercian monastery of Bellefontaine agreed to assume the responsibility of guiding and assisting this New World community, which by then numbered forty-five monks.

On October 4, 1892, fire devoured Fr. Vincent de Paul Merle's dream. Though none of the monks was injured, the monastery lay in ruins. Determined to rebuild, the monks began the work in 1894, only to be thwarted again by fire. Discouraged, some of the monks returned to Belgium and others dispersed. By 1898 only twelve monks remained. It looked as though the history of Petit Clairvaux had come to a close.

In 1899, however, the community petitioned the Order's General Chapter (or governing body) to move the monastery from Nova Scotia to the diocese of Providence, Rhode Island. In 1900, the small community relocated on three hundred stone-strewn acres and established a new monastery called Our Lady of the Valley. There they resumed monastic life and doubled in size within about ten years. Following World War II, a tidal wave of vocations swelled the size of Catholic religious orders in the United States. By 1948, Our Lady of the Valley numbered one hundred and thirty-seven monks. As did many other monasteries in the U.S., Our Lady of the Valley made a new foundation, Our Lady of Guadalupe, in New Mexico. Two years later the old enemy, fire, lashed out again. On March 21, 1950, the Solemnity of St. Benedict, the

Rhode Island monastery was destroyed, though again the monks escaped with their lives. The community of one hundred and forty monks decided to look for a new home. They found it in Spencer, Massachusetts, where they established St. Joseph's Abbey.

The community continued to grow and began making more new foundations, five between 1947 and 1960. One of those communities was established high in the Colorado Rockies in 1956. It was named St. Benedict's Monastery.

Prior to 1956, Dom Edmund Futterer, abbot of St. Joseph's Abbey, had already been considering a location on the eastern slope of the Colorado Rockies as the sight for a new monastery. At that time agriculture played the major part in Cistercian (Trappist) work and sustenance, and Dom Edmund wanted enough land to support three hundred head of cattle. However, because of an extended drought, the prospect looked discouraging on the eastern slope, and the monks began looking for land further west in Colorado's mountainous interior. In March 1954 a search party contacted a real estate agent in Grand Junction, Colorado, who directed the monks to two pieces of land, one near Snowmass and the other, called Bush Creek, further north. After looking over the Snowmass land and discovering that a road ran through the property, they passed it up and traveled north to Bush Creek. There they liked what they saw and visited the owner in Omaha, Nebraska. They were too late; another buyer had just purchased the land.

In 1955, Dom Edmund learned that land in California's Napa Valley, which he had considered for a new foundation a decade earlier, was again for sale. Stag's Leap contained one hundred and fifty acres of grape-producing land, appropriate for monastic life, as it had a ready-made industry to support it. However, the Abbey of Gethsemani in Kentucky had already purchased land for a new foundation in northern California, and the Order's General Chapter turned down Dom Edmund's request. It was reasoned that two foundations in northern California would compete for vocations. Disappointed again, Dom Edmund had to abandon the project. Today, Stag's Leap Winery produces an excellent commercial wine.

In October 1955, Dom Edmund again sent a few monks to Colorado to take another look at the Snowmass property. This time they were advised that they might be able to purchase additional land that would include the problematic road threatening the monks' privacy. (Indeed, in May 1956 they did purchase this land, securing their privacy.) The archbishop of Denver gave his blessing to the project and the Abbot General of the Order gave his approval for the foundation. Finally, the long search had ended.

On February 9, 1956, four monks from St. Joseph's Abbey arrived at the new location in Snowmass and spent the first night in an old schoolhouse about a mile down the road from the property's ranch house. The next day, the feast of St. Scholastica, they moved into the ranch house, a brick structure built around 1908, and began monastic life in the Colorado Rockies. Soon three more monks arrived, including the foundation's first superior, Fr. Leo Slatterie. With three hundred and forty-three head of cattle and a 3,100-acre ranch to maintain, they had time to make only rudimentary renovations to the ranch house, preparing for the third group of monks from St. Joseph's. They arrived on April 12, bringing the number in the community to thirteen.

The community had to face two challenges that spring. All the monks were easterners who had never lived in a semiarid climate. First, they had to tackle the job of learning how to clean and use some forty miles of ditches to irrigate six hundred acres of pastureland and six hundred acres of hayfields. The monastery's elevation of nearly eight thousand feet presented the second challenge. Used to working in Trappist mode (hard), they had to learn to slow down. This was the frequent advice of Gordon LaMoy, the rancher who had sold them the major portion of land and who was hired by the monks to teach them ranching.

A major decision had to be made before beginning construction of the new monastery. The depth of topsoil was good for agriculture but too deep to support the weight of heavy buildings. They had to use pilings to support the foundation.

In May the community purchased land adjacent to the LaMoy property, adding four hundred and eighty acres to their holdings. At the same time, twelve more monks arrived from St. Joseph's Abbey, bringing the number in the community to twenty-four. To accommodate the growing community they converted the schoolhouse into a dormitory.

In the spring of 1958, Fr. Thomas Keating, newly appointed by Dom Edmund as superior, arrived from St. Joseph's Abbey with several other monks. On November 23 of that year, the community moved into the new monastery, now substantially complete. The next morning, Sunday, Dom Edmund sang the first mass in the chapel.

Seeking an additional industry to support the community, the monks started a candy business in the spring of 1959. It was short-lived due to an

unanticipated phenomenon: made at the monastery's high elevation, the hard candy cracked when it reached lower elevations. Not to be deterred, the community decided on a new business venture of maintaining a cow calf operation. Unfortunately, this proved too much for the monks. From the proceeds of the cattle sale, they bought ten thousand chickens and built two Quonset huts to house them. In 1967, they began selling the eggs to local restaurants. The industry was a success and helped to support the community for eighteen years. It is ironic that so much time, energy and expense had gone into securing a large ranch to support a cattle operation.

In 1961, the monks at the motherhouse in Massachusetts elected Fr. Thomas as their abbot, and he had to return to St. Joseph's Abbey. As abbot of the Spencer community, he appointed their prior, Fr. Joachim Viens, to take his place as superior of St. Benedict's. Fr. Joachim served the community as superior until 1967, when Fr. Michael Abdo was appointed. By 1970, the Snowmass community had grown large and stable enough for the monastery to become an abbey in its own right, independent from the jurisdiction of their motherhouse, the founding monastery in Massachusetts. On March 31 of that year, Fr. Michael Abdo was elected the first abbot of St. Benedict's Abbey.

During the years following Vatican II (1962–1965), religious life in the United States became unsettled, and St. Benedict's, like most other religious houses, experienced a large-scale exodus of members. By 1978 there were only seven left in the community. They bonded together with dedication and kept their monastic life and witness alive through the difficult years of the 1970s, waiting for the Holy Spirit's call to bring new members.

Old farm wagon

Following the reforms of Vatican II, the Order modified its traditional emphasis on asceticism in favor of a more contemplative way of life, and permission was given for the monks to move from the traditional common dormitory into private rooms. In 1976, the community decided to build a new dorm wing of fifteen rooms—they kept alive their hope for new members—to give the monks more personal privacy. Generous benefactors made the project possible, and construction on the new dorm wing was completed late that year.

The need for new members was acute, and Dom Ambrose Southy, the Abbot General of the Order, encouraged St. Joseph's Abbey to lend them personnel. However, meeting its own needs following Vatican II presented St. Joseph's with a manpower challenge as well, and it was unable to send anyone. Nevertheless, perseverance paid off. In time St. Joseph's did send some monks, and a few of them, finding life in the Rockies at St. Benedict's to their liking, transferred to the struggling community.

During the 1970s and 1980s, the community welcomed teachers from other religious traditions. One such teacher, Maesumi Roshi, gave a workshop on the Buddhist contemplative tradition. It was a way of responding to Pope Paul VI's call to Catholic monastic communities to engage in ecumenical dialogue with Eastern religious traditions.

During the long winters the community found it difficult to celebrate early morning Vigils in the unheated church. In the autumn of 1982 they decided to insulate the church and install doors to separate it from the unheated cloister hallway. The project called for putting stucco over the original brickwork on the outside of the church. It was a trade off between aesthetics and comfort.

In 1984, having returned to St. Benedict's after serving as abbot of St. Joseph's for twenty years, Fr. Thomas Keating began an ecumenical dialogue group called the Snowmass Conference. The experiment, which included representatives from Native American, Buddhist, Hindu, Muslim, Eastern Orthodox, and Protestant traditions, continued to meet annually for the next eleven years.

Monastic life did not regain its popularity following the exodus after Vatican II, and the community created a new vocational program both to help with the work and to give men a chance to experience Cistercian life without having to make a permanent commitment. The Participant Program, begun in 1983, served this twofold purpose. It has turned out to be a success and continues to the present day, drawing men into the community for longer commitments, including three who went on to make solemn profession.

Encouraged by this stirring of new life, the community decided to convert the old dorm area into individual rooms. In August 1981 they completed the first stage of four rooms. That summer they also built a greenhouse attached to one of the Quonsets, enabling the monks to raise some of their own food as they strove to embrace the monastic tradition of providing, as far as possible, for their own needs.

During these post-Vatican II years of the Catholic Church's ecumenical thrust, Fr. William Meninger, a monk of St. Joseph's Abbey, began giving retreats based on a fourteenth-century, anonymous treatise on contemplative prayer. *The Cloud of Unknowing* presents a method for entering into deep, mystical prayer. Building on Fr. William's work, Fr. Thomas and another Spencer monk, Fr. M. Basil Pennington, began giving retreats based on this model of silent, contemplative prayer. The objective was to reclaim the tradition of contemplative prayer for Western Christianity. Because of Fr. Thomas' work in establishing Contemplative Outreach, an organization to promote a method of contemplative prayer known as Centering Prayer, St. Benedict's Monastery today serves as spiritual home for the international Centering Prayer movement, begun by these three contemplative monks.

During the 1980s, the monastery's egg industry began to experience falling prices, and when in 1984 their industry's future seemed bleak, the monks decided to phase it out and replace it with a small bakery for making cookies. On May 9, 1986, they began selling cookies to local supermarkets.

In April 1985, after serving the community as superior for eighteen years, Fr. Michael stepped down as abbot, and on May 29 the community elected Fr. Joseph Boyle. On July 11, the Solemnity of St. Benedict, Auxiliary Bishop Dominic Marconi of Newark, New Jersey, bestowed the Church's official blessing on the community's new abbot.

Fire, the old archenemy, struck again on April 22, 1986. The spring cleaning of irrigation ditches included the burning of brush that had accumulated over the winter. One such burning went out of control for two hours, consuming a hayshed and a delivery truck and damaging a tractor.

By October of that year, work to convert the old dorm into individual rooms was complete, and the small community had room to accommodate twenty-five people. In the autumn of 1987 this growing community began meeting with Diane Fassel, a professional group facilitator, in order to improve the monks' skills in communicating with one another. The venture proved to be a blessing, and the community has continued the meetings for eighteen years.

On May 31, 1991, the monks reelected Fr. Joseph as their abbot, and in July, addressing their need for new retreat facilities, they met for the first time with architects from the Aspen firm of Conger and Fuller. Plans were drawn up, and fundraising began. Through the generosity of benefactors, the monks, unable themselves to construct the new facilities, hired a contractor, and construction got underway. On October 18, 1992, the monks gathered with benefactors and held the traditional groundbreaking and blessing ceremony. On February 12, 1993, when the builders finished the framework for the top of the first building, the community and construction crew celebrated a traditional "topping off" party.

The next year, concerned about the pace of housing and commercial development in the area, the monks joined with three other adjacent large landowners to insure protection from developers. They attempted an agreement to keep their combined 10,000 or more acres rural and agricultural. Due to inevitable complexities, ten years of legal negotiations ended with no resolution.

After four years of fundraising and construction, the new retreat house became a reality, and on July 11, 1995, it was consecrated. In perfect weather, about ninety invited donors helped to celebrate the conclusion of what had been thirty years of discussions and planning for a new facility. The last four years had made the new retreat house a reality. It was a successful project in more ways than one. The effort created a retreat house, which caught the attention of the American Institute of Architects which, in 1996, singled it out for excellence in religious architecture that year.

In 1996, the monks were able to celebrate Fr. Thomas' fiftieth anniversary of profession, an event to which their motherhouse, St. Joseph's Abbey, sent two monks to represent the community he had led for twenty years.

In 1997, the community reelected Fr. Joseph as abbot and stipulated that he remain in that office indefinitely rather than for the usual term of six years. This decision was not only a vote of confidence in his effective leadership, but also an expression of the monks' love and respect for him personally.

The monks had one more pressing issue to address. As a young community, they had not experienced a pressing need for rooms to accommodate the sick and elderly. An older community now, the time had

come to provide assisted living quarters. They hired two of the architects who had worked on the retreat house and began a fundraising campaign. Friends again responded generously. The new wing took a year of noisy, dust-filled construction to build, but shortly before Christmas 2000 it was ready for occupancy.

In October 1998, during one of its communications workshops with Diane Fassel, the community addressed the task of creating a vision statement. Reflecting on their own lives and the monastery's purpose, they drew up the following: "Through daily life in our Cistercian community, we aspire to be transformed in mind and heart by embodying Christ Jesus in ways appropriate to our times."

In the opening years of the twenty-first century, the community celebrated two more fiftieth anniversaries; in 2003 Br. Benito Williamson, and in 2004 Br. John Collins celebrated fifty years of vows in the monastic life. At the same time, the community experienced the need for more priests since no monk had been ordained for more than thirty years, and only three priests remained in its ranks. In May 2004 they called two brothers to the priesthood. On July 11, 2005, exactly twenty years after he had blessed Fr. Joseph as abbot, Bishop Dominic Marconi ordained Brothers Charles Albanese and Micah Schonberger to the priesthood. The community again looks to the future with faith in God's providence and an openness to embrace his will.

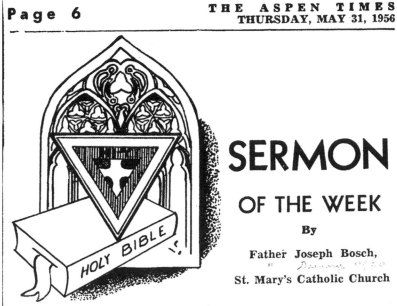

SERMON

OF THE WEEK

By

Father Joseph Bosch,

St. Mary's Catholic Church

THE TRAPPISTS

The Cistercian Monks of the Strict Observance (Trappists) have acquired property in Snowmass where they intend to erect a monastery of their Order. The project is under the direction of the Rt. Rev. M. Edmund Futterer, O.S.C.O., Abbot of Saint Joseph's Abbey in Spencer, Massachusetts.

Founded in the eleventh century, stemming from the ancient Order of Saint Benedict, and following his rule, the Cistercians are today one of the few contemplative Orders of men in the Catholic Church. they are strictly enclosed, separated from all apostolic work such as preaching or teaching, and devoted to a life of prayer and penance, of silence and manual labor.

Their chief duty is the singing of the Divine Office in choir at the appointed hours, and to this nothing must be preferred. They rise at 2:00 A.M. each morning for Matins and Lauds, and frequently during the day they return to church to sing the other hours of the Divine Office.

Manual labor has always been held in great esteem by the Cistercians and forms an essential part of the lives of both the Choir religious and the lay brothers. Agriculture and the rearing of cattle are the traditional means of support in all Cistercian houses. The group at Snowmass will continue to manage the beef herd on the ranch they have acquired.

Taking literally the injunction of Christ that, to be perfect, a man must sell all, give to the poor, and follow Him, young men from every walk of life leave home and family and friends to dedicate their lives to God within the walls of a Cistercian monastery. There, in deep peace and joy they learn the truth of the saying "All the way to Heaven is Heaven, for He said 'I am the Way'". The Cistercian life is a life "hidden away with Christ in God", a life of prayer and reparation and thanksgiving.

There are presently twenty-four religious at the new foundation in Snowmass—fourteen lay brothers and ten choir religious, of whom five are priests. They expect to begin construction of the new monastery immediately. In the late fall or early spring they hope to have accommodations for visiting priests or lay men who wish to spend a few days in quiet retirement at the monastery.

Letters From the People

Some History

Editor: I read with considerable interest Marranzino's recent series of articles about the Trappist Monastery near Snowmass.

I am intimately acquainted with that part of the state for that valley and that old brick ranch house were my home for more than half of my life. Dad and mother raised a family of five, a girl and four boys, two of us born in that house, built by my grandfather; and two married there.

It is 20 years since I dressed in one of those upstairs rooms before going to Aspen and my own marriage and to establish my own home.

My mother's people settled that valley in the early 1880s and mother herself went there as a child of about 7 following the death of her own mother, and she was raised by Mr. and Mrs. Henry Staats, an uncle and aunt.

Henry Staats located and patented the land where the new monastery is being built. He was also one of the original group who wintered in Aspen in 1879-80.

Mr. Staats and Aunt Ella, for whom mother was named, sold their holdings and departed for Eastern Colorado about 1909.

Another aunt, Columbia Harmon, and two brothers of hers and Mrs. Staats, Herbert and Amos Harmon, also had early filings.

My grandfather, Charles Hart, bought the Columbia Harmon land and the D-H brand from Dennis Hughes about 1897 and it was he who built the brick home and the big barn on that property.

Dad went to the ranch at that time as a youth and lived there the greater part of the ensuing 38 years until he and mother sold to the Lamoy family.

That valley was named 70 years or more ago, Capitol Park. I realize that a new name may be required by the new residents, but the old one stood a long time.

I sincerely hope the Brothers will succeed in their undertakings down there and know they will find true peace and quiet and imagine their eyes will turn west to "Old Sopris" in the dawn and again as evening shadows descend as have the eyes of all who preceded them in that setting.

The gardeners among them will find that most hardy vegetables thrive and grow exceedingly in thrive and grow exceedingly well in that soil. Carrots, beets, peas, rutabagas and green beans if a late frost doesn't nip the tender plants. CHARLES D. HART
Laramie, Wyo.

Old ranching homestead now used as a hermitage for monks' retreats